CASEY JONES

Adapted by
Stephen Krensky

Illustrations by
Mark Schroder

On My Own

FOLKLORE

M Millbrook Press/Minneapolis

Text copyright © 2007 by Stephen Krensky
Illustrations copyright © 2007 by Lerner Publishing Group, Inc.

Millbrook Press, Inc.
A division of Lerner Publishing Group, Inc.
241 First Avenue North
Minneapolis, MN 55401 U.S.A.

Website address: www.lernerbooks.com

Library of Congress Cataloging-in-Publication Data

Krensky, Stephen.
  Casey Jones / by Stephen Krensky ; illustrations by Mark Schroder.
     p.   cm. — (On my own folklore)
    ISBN-13: 978–1–57505–890–0 (lib. bdg. : alk. paper)
    ISBN-10: 1–57505–890–1 (lib. bdg. : alk. paper)
    1. Jones, Casey, 1863–1900—Juvenile literature.   2. Locomotive engineers—United
States—Biography—Juvenile literature.   I. Schroder, Mark.   II. Title.   III. Series:
Krensky, Stephen. On my own folklore.
  TJ603.5.Q56K74 2007
  385.36092—dc22   2005032536

Manufactured in the United States of America
2 3 4 5 6 7 – DP – 12 11 10 09 08 07

For James E. Storer
—SK

To my wife, Nicole,
and daughter, Anya
—MS

Casey Jones: A Folklore Hero

Maybe you have heard of Casey Jones. Perhaps someone has mentioned his name, or you have heard a story or song. Casey Jones is one of America's tall tale heroes. Stories about him come to us from the men who worked the railroad in the late 1800s. Some of these men were firemen. They shoveled coal into the boiler of steam engines to make the trains run. Some were telegraphers, who sent and received messages. Others were engineers. They drove the trains. Casey was one of the greatest train engineers of his time.

We call stories like Casey's tall tales because everything in them is extra big, extra fast, and extra wild. And the truth in these stories might be just a bit stretched. The heroes and heroines in tall tales are as tall as buildings, as strong as oxen, or as fast as lightning. They meet with wild adventures at every turn. But that's okay, because they can solve just about every problem that comes their way.

Tall tales may be funny and outsized. But they describe the life that many workers and pioneers shared. The people in these stories have jobs that real people had. And the stories were always set in familiar places.

The first tellers of these tales may have known these people and places. Or they may have wished they could be just like the hero in the story. The stories were told again and again and passed from person to person. We call such spoken and shared stories folklore.

Folklore is the stories and customs of a place or a people. Folklore can be folktales like the tall tale. These stories are usually not written down until much later, after they have been told and retold for many years. Folklore can also be sayings, jokes, and songs.

Folklore can teach us something. A rhyme or a song may help us remember an event from long ago. Or it may be just for fun, such as a good ghost story or a jump-rope song. Folklore can also tell us about the people who share the stories.

Casey Jones was a real person. He took on inventions such as the telegraph and the steam locomotive. His biggest challenge, however, came the morning of April 30, 1900, when he was trying to get a late train back on schedule. Tales of his brave actions that morning quickly spread up and down the rails. His deeds live on in the many versions of "The Ballad of Casey Jones."

Getting Started

Casey Jones liked to be on time.

He made this clear

right from the start.

As his birth neared,

his parents wondered

when he would make his first appearance.

They needn't have worried.

He wasn't born a day early

or a day late.

He appeared right on time.

Of course, he wasn't Casey Jones then.

He was John Luther Jones.

But he grew up in Cayce, Kentucky,

and the name Casey stuck to him later

like soot on a smokestack.

There was no question that little Casey
had a certain way about him.
When he was hungry,
he cried every four minutes
until he was fed.
No more and no less.
Neighbors could set their clocks
by his nap times.
Every afternoon, he fell asleep at 2:00
and woke up exactly two hours later.
Even when he was ill,
Casey kept track of things.
When he got the 24-hour flu,
he wasn't sick
a minute more than necessary.

Casey kept an ear out for roosters too.

If any of them crowed

even a second after sunrise,

he tracked them down

and gave them a piece of his mind.

As Casey grew, his habits grew with him.

When his mother called for dinner,

Casey was already sitting in his seat,

his napkin tucked under his chin.

At school, Casey always arrived first.

Then he rang the bell

so the other students

would hurry up and move along.

Casey was a happy child,

but one thing bothered him mightily.

Why didn't the sun rise and set

at the same time every day?

People tried to explain it to him,

but Casey just shook his head.

As far as he was concerned,

the sun was being stubborn.

But it was so far away,

there was nothing he could do about it.

In his free time,
Casey would go down by the river
to see the trains swap cargoes
with the ferryboats.
Where were those big crates going?
And where had they been?

Casey never tired of watching
all the commotion.
There was something about it
that drew him like a nail to a magnet.

Building Up Steam

At 15, Casey got a job
as a telegrapher for the railroad.
He would tap out messages
and send them over the wire.
Nobody could beat Casey for speed.
His hand moved so fast that
some people swore he had
a few extra fingers helping out.
All those dots and dashes
knew better than to dally
after they left his fingertips.
If they didn't start fast enough
down the wire,
Casey was likely to chase after them,
yelling all the way.

Every day, Casey watched
the trains roar by.
He noted their progress
for other stations down the line.
When the trains were on time,
Casey smiled
and whistled while he worked.
When they were late,
he gritted his teeth
and kicked over the wastebasket.

After three years, Casey decided
that the trains could use his help
to stay on time.
So he became a fireman,
stoking a boiler
on a steam locomotive.

His real goal was to be an engineer
and drive a train.
It was the engineer, after all,
who made sure the train arrived on time.
There were jokes about a man
who once took a slow train
on his first day of work.

Well, that train was so pokey
that the man had to retire
before he got home that night.
Casey Jones wasn't going to be driving
any trains like that.

Finally, at the age of 26,

Casey completed his training

and became an engineer himself.

He was so tall, though,

that he couldn't stand up in the cab.

So he spent a lot of time

with his head stuck out the window.

Some folks reckoned a giraffe

might have looked the same.

Casey didn't care what they said.

He was proud of his new job.

And his wife Janie said

his new uniform fit him well.

Casey was so good-looking

that mirrors lined up for the chance

to show his reflection.

Now Casey's wife was his first love.

But his second

was his company's new steam engine.

With two pilot wheels

and eight drive wheels,

it was known as a 2-8-0.

Casey first saw it

at the Chicago World's Fair in 1893.

When the fair ended,

Casey showed up with papers

claiming the engine for himself.

For the next seven years,

Casey and that engine

were always together on the rails.

Riding the Rails

Every engineer had a whistle
in his cab.
Sometimes he pulled it as a warning.
Sometimes he pulled it as a greeting.
And sometimes he pulled it
because he happened to be in the mood.
The whistles screamed or screeched
or squealed or wailed.
Casey's whistle was something special.
It was a six-tone whistle
made of long and short tubes
banded together.
Casey's most famous call
sounded like the song of a whip-poor-will.
But whatever tune he played,
it was always recognized along the tracks.

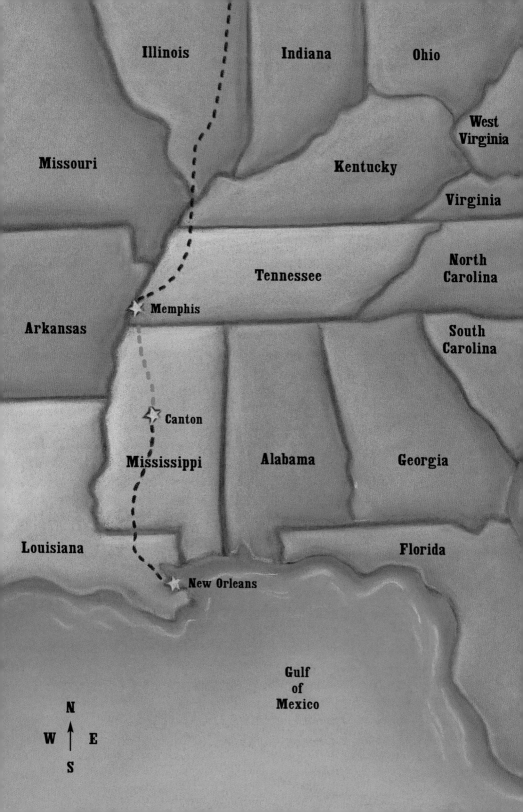

Casey blew that whistle long and loud
the day he was promoted
to drive the New Orleans Special.
His route covered 188 miles—
from Memphis, Tennessee,
to Canton, Mississippi.
The New Orleans Special
was also known as the Cannonball.
Casey liked the name just fine.
Nobody ever talked about cannonballs
arriving late.
And if he had his way,
nobody would ever talk about him
arriving late either.

There was a story of one train

that never arrived at a station late.

This train went so fast

that the rails melted underneath it

and the railroad ties burned behind it.

But one day that train

went roaring up a hill,

outrunning the wind.

At the top of the hill,

the tracks went back down,

but that train just kept going up.

Right into the air it flew,

up toward space.

Some people claim it's running there still.

Casey's train never ran as fast as that.

He took pride in being a safe driver.

No passenger had ever been injured

when he was in charge.

One night, Casey found some news
waiting for him at his last stop.
The engineer scheduled to do
the return route was sick.
Could Casey take his place?
Casey said that he could.
Oh, there was one more thing.
That train was running late.
Casey wasn't worried.
He wouldn't melt the tracks,
but he could push the train along
fast enough.

The Last Run

The schedule called for the late train

to be back on time

when it reached Canton, Mississippi.

That meant making up 95 minutes

in 188 miles.

Casey thought he was up

to the challenge.

In the first 100 miles,

he gained back a full hour.

"Only 35 minutes behind,"

he told his fireman.

"The old girl's got her high-heeled

slippers on tonight."

After another 23 miles,

the train was only 15 minutes late.

But there was trouble ahead.

As the train approached one little depot,

some freight cars were blocking the tracks.

Somehow, Casey and his fireman

didn't see the lantern's warning signal.

So when they came by the last bend,

the Cannonball was still going

70 miles an hour.

"Look out!" said the fireman.

"We're going to hit something!"

Casey told the fireman to jump,

and jump he did,

tumbling safely to the ground.

Casey stayed behind.

If he jumped, he might save himself.

But what would happen to the crew

and passengers on board?

Casey wasn't about to leave them,

not if there was even the smallest chance

of stopping the train.

Well, the brakes squealed so loud
they sounded like a pig
with its tail caught in a keyhole.
70 . . . 60 . . . 55 miles an hour.
The train was straining every bolt and rivet,
trying its best to stop.
But there wasn't enough room
or enough time.
The big 10-wheel locomotive
tore through the freight cars
on the tracks ahead
before finally crashing to a stop.
It was very good luck
that no one was on board those freight cars.
But that luck didn't hold for Casey.

Because he stayed at his post,
the Cannonball had slowed
as much as possible.
No one else on board was badly hurt.
Brave Casey had saved them all.
But Casey took the collision head-on
and was killed in the crash.

Casey Jones is gone now.

But some people say

he still keeps an eye on the trains

crisscrossing the countryside.

On a clear night,

you may hear a train whistle in the distance.

But there's no train to be seen.

That's Casey.

When a train arrives at a station,

he blows once on his own private whistle.

And then he moves on,

always checking to see

if the trains arrive on time.

Further Reading and Websites

American Folklore
http://www.americanfolklore.net
This folklore website feature tall tales, ghost stories, regional legends, and famous characters.

Balkwill, Richard. *The Best Book of Trains*. New York: Kingfisher Books, 1999. Learn about the history of the railroad, different types of trains, and how they work.

Casey Jones Home and Railroad Museum
http://www.caseyjones.com/pages/serv01.htm
Find out more about Casey, his legend, and his home in Jackson, Tennessee.

Casey Jones—The Real Story
http://www.watervalley.net/users/caseyjones/casey.htm
This site from the Water Valley Casey Jones Railroad Museum has the most complete information on Casey Jones's life, the accident, and the people involved. You can also find photographs and the lyrics to songs about Casey.

Farmer, Nancy. *Casey Jones's Fireman: The Story of Sim Webb*. New York: Phyllis Fogelman Books, 1998. Sim Webb, Casey Jones's real-life fireman the morning of the accident, is the main character in this fictional tale of Casey's whistle.

Johnson, Angela. *I Dream of Trains*. New York: Simon & Schuster Books for Young Readers, 2003. An African American boy dreams of a better life on the railroad like his hero Casey Jones.

Wroble, Lisa A. *Kids during the Industrial Revolution*. New York: PowerKids Press, 1999. The author describes what life was like for children during the Industrial Revolution.